Part self-development, part confessional - journalist Meghan Bunchman is pulling back the curtain of the TV news industry by sharing TV tips and secrets that you've always wondered about. Because who doesn't want to hear about the TV world's best kept secrets?!

Synopsis

Part self-development, part confessional - journalist Meghan Bunchman is pulling back the curtain of the TV news industry to share television tips and secrets that you've always wondered about. Because who doesn't want to hear about who does our makeup or what our work day really looks like.

The perfect quick read for every woman looking to hone her voice. From new grads entering the workforce to CEOs of multimillion-dollar companies, *Broadcast YOUR Beauty* teaches you how to own your beauty, words and worth from the inside out.

Dedication

For every woman who's ever
doubted her worth:
You are powerful!

ISBN 978-1-61808-184-1

Printed in the United States of America

White Feather Press

Reaffirming Faith in God, Family, and Country!

BROADCAST YOUR BEAUTY

*-TV tips and secrets for
your real world self-*

Meghan Anne Bunchman

Contents

Introduction

It doesn't matter what industry you work in - from media to software engineering to financial planning - everyone can agree strong verbal and nonverbal communication skills are pivotal to your career growth. But here's the thing … as a woman in the work world we (at some point in our careers) will be forced into situations that are unfair, uncomfortable and inappropriate. We'll be reprimanded for our unique voices, taught to question our worth, and for lack of a better description forced to lessen ourselves to make others feel comfortable. What's even worse is that at some point you might start believing these lies. I'm here to tell you that's not okay and I can help!

You shouldn't have to change or alter yourself to make others feel better. You shouldn't be exposed to a world of systemic sexism where descriptions like "argumentative," "difficult," and (dare I say) "bitch" are associated with your strong, female voice. You shouldn't experience a workplace that teaches you women are meant to be seen and not heard. You shouldn't have to question your worth, beauty and value, because no one will give you the time of day. We shouldn't have these shared experiences and yet … we all will.

So, as an experienced journalist, I'm here to share with you some of my more embarrassing and awkward on-air experiences and ideally teach you how to successfully navigate your own life by finding your inner confidence. In my world of TV news, sexism and superficial stereotypes are a very real thing.

....

From internal management style,
to viewers expectations, female
news reporters are expected to
look like Marilyn Monroe, talk like
Michelle Obama, sacrifice like Betty
Draper and smile like Jackie Onassis.
What does that mean? "In short,
the TV news world is a modern-day
version of a superficial *Hunger Games*."

....

Meghan Anne Bunchman

A female anchor needs to be sexy, but not slutty. We're expected to be smart, but not a know-it-all. People expect us to be educated, but not elitist. Our hair needs to be coiffed. Our eyeliner the perfect degree of smudged, and our voice strong, but not too assertive.

These expectations seem impossible to live up to and at times, they are. I'm never going to say I'm always on my game. I'm not going to lie to you and say my journey has been flawless, because that is not realistic. What is realistic - and I hope relatable - is vulnerability. Sharing my own experiences through trial-and-error, so that you can avoid the same pitfalls I've already stumbled through. It's not about changing yourself to fit the mold others press upon you. It's about doubling down and having so much confidence in yourself that your own unique style shines. Plus, who doesn't want to learn about that perfect eyelash curl, designer dress and TV hair?

I'm not saying I'm an expert by any means, but I am experienced and honest. In fact, I've been in the world of TV news for more than a decade. I've persevered through a huge industry shift when the recession hit, and I came out on top. I've covered military movement from the Hill and the White House. I've broken national news stories, including when a now-convicted murderer went on a shooting spree while picking up Uber riders. I've documented the beautiful and heartbreaking journey of a Chicago 6th grader who returned to her inner-city school as a female. All to endure criticism from both her peers and administration as she started the process of gender transitioning. And I've even had one-on-one interviews with presidential candidates. What I'm saying is that I've been tried and tested. I've felt small or not worthy at some points (because that's what I had been told) and yet somehow I rose up to the challenge and so can you!

In addition to anchoring daily newscasts, I also teach journalism at a local university. My students like to joke that I look their age, but I just chalk that up to Botox, because dang, my now-covered-up worry lines have stories to tell.

Most of my students aren't even looking to work in the world of media. However, they are smart enough to know that editing skills, strong communication and speech-delivery techniques are pivotal to landing their first job. So, I teach them how to refine their point through stature, presentation and voice. And I hope to do the same for you with *Broadcast YOUR Beauty*.

No, this book isn't one of your boring college reads. It's funny, humiliating and just the right amount of girly. It's meant to be a fast beachside read that (IMHO) is always best accompanied with a chilled glass of rosé. Here I'll teach you all the TV hair and makeup tricks you've always wondered about, and even share with you some of the news world's dirty, little secrets. Once we've perfected your external confidence, then the real work will begin ... broadcasting your value.

We'll discuss powerful presentation skills, finding your voice, identifying your key demographic and owning your worth. Some of the chapters even have a call-to-action at the end. So, keep your pens ready!

....

Do the work now, so that you
can reap the benefits for
a lifetime to come.

....

TV Wardrobe

"She wore that dress already this month"

DO YOU REMEMBER A COUPLE of years back when "the dress" was circulating the internet? No, not the "is it blue or gold" dress, but the TV News dress. Remember: that pop of broadcast brightness with black, figure-flattering panels along the sides of the bodice? Well, here's the reason that dress popped up on meteorologists, anchors and reporters across every market in the states: it's cheap! As in only $30 on Amazon.

Let me let you in on the first of many secrets: unless you are a Hoda Kotb or a Megyn Kelly of the world, TV news reporters make very little. WHAT? I can't believe that, you say. That's all relative, you argue. True. But let's put this into perspective. A reporter who works in a midsize city -let's say Green Bay, Wisconsin (who, by the way forfeits countless weekends and holidays with their families to bring you the "latest news) is typically paid between 26-30k. Then add a big budget for "TV makeup" and broadcast clothing, and you can bet most news girls are BFFs with bargain shopping.

Here's another scenario for you. Viewers have a double standard for male vs. female reporters. (But doesn't society, really?) Don't believe me? Well, stop what you're doing right now and google "TV anchor wears same suit for a year." Seriously, put down this book for a second and watch that video … I'll wait.

Welcome back. In case you didn't view the video let me summarize it for you: an Australian male news anchor proves a point about inherent biases us (as viewers) apply to men and women within my field by wearing - you guessed it - the same suit for an entire year. During this trial, his female counterpart brightly lights up a TV montage through a wide array of dress styles and colors. The male anchor notes not a single viewer called him out on his experiment, but you better believe if a woman on TV wore the same dress - even just weeks apart - someone is sliding into her DMs, criticizing her wardrobe choice. Believe me. It's happened to me … several times. So, what's the point of this story? Well, women on TV aren't well compensated (or women in general, frankly) and yet they have to dress to a higher standard.

That's where Amazon, Forever 21, Pretty Little Things and other online retailers come in.

....

Time to share some TV tips and tricks
... think bright!

....

As someone who virtually lives in a white tank and leather jacket in my off time, my wardrobe may look a bit bipolar. Especially because in the broadcast world, color is king ... or should I say queen!

Tip number one:

While on-air bright, solid colors are always the most flattering. But before you run out and start buying Barbie's dream wardrobe, you'll need to learn your tones. For me (a pale-skinned blonde) royal colors work best: rich blues, vibrant pinks and emerald greens. For some of my friends who are blessed with olive undertones: pale pinks and yellows are standouts on them. The important thing to take away from this is to keep that bright, complementary color on at least the top half of your body. Why? Because your eyes glimmer a bit differently and your hair color will pop.

Tip number two:

Avoid prints (at least at work.) Prints are not always figure flattering and may garner the wrong type of attention. I mean, you don't want someone staring at you for an uncomfortable period of time, trying to figure out if that floral was meant to hit directly on your chest, right? For on-camera work, prints can come off blurry and confusing - especially if the reporter is in-studio with all of the strong lighting or in front of a green screen, or even when you're presenting a project in a boardroom or on stage. Prints are great for days by the pool or picnics in the park, but for your everyday wardrobe be bold and rock a bright solid.

It's also important to know that a lot of female anchors have really cornered the market with Rent the Runway's monthly subscription. Although I have never used Rent the Runway myself, here's what I know about this little gem. For a monthly subscription of about $150 per month you can borrow four pieces at a time to wear, then send them back and select four more. Shipping and dry cleaning are built into this price. A lot of anchors I know who use RtR love it. They get a wardrobe with variety and actually find themselves spending less on clothing. Less. Do you hear me: less! Crazy, right?

Then there are also the pieces that we need for off-the-air events. It's built into our contracts that "talent" or on-air reporters and anchors are required to go to specific parades, charity events and media nights each year. Which events depend on where you live and the station you work for. But for real; they are mandatory. I missed a parade once in my early days, and you better believe I was called in to my boss's office the next week for a stern talking to. (Also, it's important to note that we aren't paid extra for these appearances.)

Speaking of appearances, anchors and reporters are often invited to emcee additional galas around town or to be keynote speakers for high schools and sports team graduations. Sure, we can wear a standard on-air dress sometimes, but, for more formal occasions, cocktail dresses or even black-tie gowns may be required. Thus, the added advantage of Rent the Runway and its wide variety from work attire to gowns. Even if you're not a subscription-likely consumer, I have several friends who swear by renting the one-off piece for weddings and big events. I SWEAR this is not sponsored. Hah! But I wanted to share with you more secrets of the news world that perhaps you may have never thought about or heard of before.

Now back to us frugal buyers. Before I give you a list of awesome Amazon finds (again not sponsored) I want to hit on the point of "knowing your body type." No, not just knowing … but embracing your body type. Ready for me to spill some more TV tea?

Every station I've ever worked at has brought in (from time-to-time) some sort of consultant to, in theory, fine-tune on-air talents' style, delivery and/or makeup look. It's not uncommon or unheard of to spend the day at a mall with this so-called consultant. Or perhaps you brought in twenty outfits for he or she to review. I get it. Sometimes that voice in our head or BFFs aren't telling us the truth about our wardrobe, so cue the consultant. With that said, in my humble opinion a consultant is going to get a lot further with a bit of honey rather than vinegar. However, in my experience the vinegar consultant tends to show up more often than not.

One of the consultants I was so blessed to experience falls into that latter category. I'm not being cheeky, "blessed" is the correct word, because that experience opened my eyes. Anyways, call me old fashioned, but I think it's important for a consultant to have something called qualifications. In this instance, the woman who was brought in to "image consult" with us had amazing personal style, but no clue about on-air dressing and dressing for different body types.

Cut to our shopping day: a group of four on-air women standing in the middle of a Macy's fitting room in items we'd never feel comfortable wearing on or off-air and this woman pressuring us to buy them. With no regards to each of our own insecurities, trouble areas, post pregnancy bodies or budgets. In fact, at one point this consultant (with a full smile on her face) even admitted that she likes to push people to their limits just to see if they'd break. From personal experience she wasn't just talking about pushing people to their clothing comfort limit.

Broadcast YOUR Beauty

....

News flash:
being a bitch isn't cool!
But I digress.

....

One of the on-air women I was with that day is blessed with a womanly body, which includes a full chest. (Lucky her, I'm still praying mine will come in one day, or maybe I'll just buy them.) Anyways, she is top heavy with the most beautiful thin legs. In this case, our consultant kept putting her in skin-tight dresses that were nearing bodycon style (save that for Vegas and bachelorette parties) and polka dots. Lots and lots of polka dots?! Big mistake. Big. Huge. (I have to go shopping now.) Remember when I said that you should avoid all prints on TV because they don't read well on camera and studio lighting can reflect prints strangely? Yep. That's basically a major no-no for TV news dressing 101. As for the bodycon style dresses - although my dear friend looked incredible in them, she didn't feel comfortable. Typically, if you are blessed with boobs you want to balance out that shape on your bottom half. Try a fit and flare or classic skater-style skirt. You'll be able to achieve that perfect hour-glass figure and feel far more comfortable.

....

It's always important to remember
to dress for your body type ...
the body you have now, not
the body you want or once had.

....

Another friend of mine who was with us that day - the most conservative in the group - had just had a baby. So, she too had a fuller chest. Our consultant kept putting her in low-cut tops, which anyone could see was incredibly uncom-fortable for my friend to wear. I mean, she looked beautiful and sexy. But no matter how good an outfit looks on you, if you don't feel comfortable in it, you're never going to be able to rock it. The consultant kept pressuring her to buy item after item that my friend was never going to wear. In the end, my friend (and to be honest most of the people who were "heavily-encouraged" to shop with this said consultant) bought the items and intentionally kept the receipts. We all learned it was much easier to let this woman think she was getting her way and return the items after she left. Oh, did I mention that most of us spent 400-600 dollars of our own money. As in that day we were pressured (read: bullied) into wearing items that the station wasn't willing to pay for itself.

Then there was my experience. Remember when I said I'm still praying for my boobs to come in? Well I'm 30 and still waiting … in the meantime Victoria's Secret and Spanx are my close friends. I mean who doesn't love that bra that adds two cup sizes! Hello Bs! I used to joke with the floor saleswomen that I wear a DD … inverted. As for my womanly body, well I'm still praying and waiting for that too. I'm as straight as a pre-pubescent teen. No shape. No chest. No one standout feature to highlight. Thus, the need for Spanx to create shape. My dear friend who works in Chicago let me in on a little secret a couple of years back called the Squeem. An awesome Amazon purchase that's basically a Spanx corset. Strap that baby on me and voila, I have a waist and curves! Just be careful when you first start wearing this baby … breathing becomes a challenge. (I wish I was kidding.)

Meghan Anne Bunchman

So, when the consultant decided it was my turn to be her target (uh … focus) her clothing pieces were confusing at best. First, she kept trying to find things that would fit me. She'd pull 0s and 00s left and right and those pieces would fall right off of me. I'm not saying I am skinny, skinny. But clothing sizing within the states has become distorted. I have a whole theory on why, but I'll save that for another book or at least an article in a national publication (*Conde Nast*, hit me up)! Then she started pulling tops with a lot going on up top. As in bows and bling and ruffles. Um, no thank you. Even with a smaller-framed body, adding dimension to your shoulders will inevitably make anyone look like a linebacker. What should have been pulled for me are pieces with cinched waistlines and belts. Belts galore. If you don't have a waist, then you have to create one visually through color blocking. Also, call me crazy, but resort wear dresses aren't appropriate when anchoring non-stop coverage of a school shooting or political funeral. Just saying.

Some of my favorite buys...

Amazon Squeem

Remember that torture device I was talking about a moment ago that gives my boy-like-body some shape? The Squeem 'Perfect Waist' Contouring Cincher is described as shapewear that achieves a seamless, smooth and shapely curves you (I guess in this case, that's me) desire without sacrificing comfort. In all actuality, the first couple of times I wore this baby under my dresses I experienced extreme discomfort. I'm talking side effect of hangry-like symptoms. No, I wasn't actually hungry, just incredibly uncomfortable. In hindsight maybe I should have ordered a size up, but oh well. Anyways after a couple of wears and washes this corset has become my safety blanket. For real. There's probably something wrong with me, because I find myself being the most relaxed when I'm sucked in. I mean, isn't that why high-waisted yoga pants are so popular right now? The fact is shapewear can be a lifesaver for special events or when you've had just a few too many cocktails.

Meghan Anne Bunchman

"The Dress"

Yep, the same dress I was talking about at the beginning of this book. The Homeyee_dress comes in a dozen "broadcast bright" colors and has perfectly placed black paneling along the sides to emphasize a more hourglass shape. The dress is less than $30 and is figure flattering on all body types. It's funny because this dress (IMHO) was the gateway dress for on-air talent. All of a sudden we, as anchors and reporters, realized how much money we were wasting on brand-name attire that takes a beating thanks to heavy tripods, lighting and cameras. The dress's online description even points out that more than 60 meteorologists have been seen wearing this dress.

Purple Asymmetrical Dress

From business attire to cocktail events, Amazon really has everything. This little gem I've worn both on-air and at hosting gigs. I love the simple asymmetrical detail that makes it look more expensive than it really is (only $28)! Honestly, I could go on and on about the dozen Amazon buys I have in my closet for work, but this is supposed to be a quick read. So instead let me just list some of the brands, and you can go down the Amazon search rabbit hole later.

Miusol
Homeyee
Woosea
Vfshow
Woosunze

Why do I love these brands? Because they're cheap - as in affordable. But the material is the right weight and a strong enough cotton blend that wears well, stretches and has a shelf life of more than three washes.

Meghan Anne Bunchman

A Picture Perfect Face

"Girl, add some lashes"

DO YOU HAVE MAKEUP ARTISTS helping you in the morning? That's probably one of the most common questions I hear when people find out I'm a news anchor and/or field reporter. And the short answer to this is NO. Unless you're in a very large city (think Dallas, D.C., LA or Chicago) the answer is no. Even in those cities, typically only anchors get makeup help. Want to know another secret: only about a third of TV stations give their reporters and anchors a clothing, hair and/or makeup allowance. What does that mean? Well, most of your on-air talent are paying out of their own pocket to keep up their "TV look." The kicker, if that said reporter started letting her grey hairs grow out or maybe stopped applying those false lashes every day,

23

they'd likely be called into the News Director's office to talk about their appearance.

....

By the way - men are not held to the same standard. It's another double standard in our world, both from the management perspective and viewer's expectations.

....

(But more of that later.) We, as TV news women, are expected to keep up our on-air look and style, but again aren't typically compensated for that.

Now that we've addressed the assumptions or expectations of female news anchors, it's time for me to share my tricks with you on how to look your best for less! Brows. Brows, brows, brows. As a pale-skinned blonde, if I don't wear mascara and pencil in my eyebrows people think I'm sick. Like actually sick. Not because I didn't put in the effort, but because I really have no defining feature on my face, and I just look sallow. If only I had discovered the power of strong eyebrows in my youth … (sigh) I would have saved myself hours of "untagging" or photoshopping unflattering photos.

Meghan Anne Bunchman

Even if you are blessed to have darker hair, a strong and defined eyebrow is a game changer. They frame your face. For me personally, I'm an Anastasia lover. The line offers eyebrow stencils. (yes, actual stencils!) that I use to first add powder and definition to my brows, and then I follow up with an eyebrow wiz pencil to elongate the tip of the brow. Then there are lashes, which have become more mainstream in the past couple of years. But before the trend of lash extensions, I'd say about three quarters of female reporters used falsies. Now some have hopped on the extension train, but the result is the same. Why? Because eyes show emotion and lashes open up the face. Many use strip lashes, but I've seen some ladies commit to the tedious work of adding individual lashes for a more natural look. But let's be honest, if you see a reporter or anchor out in the field … nothing about them looks natural. We're enhanced, baked, contoured and sucked within an inch of our lives. Okay I'm being a bit dramatic, but there is a lot of smoke and mirrors.

Lighting

Lighting matters. Period. Whether you're in studio breaking a national story or taking a fabulous selfie on your whirlwind trip to Thailand,

The Golden Hour

It's actually the golden hours: as in the two hours in the day that natural lighting is pure perfection. The actual time will vary depending on where you live, but the two hours fall just after the sun rises and just before it sets. The sun's color is at its peak warmth – the most flattering tone for all skin tones. Plus the shadows are long and lean. Taking a picture at high noon tends to result in an unfortunate Groucho Marx like shadow mustache and raccoon shadow under eyes.

lighting can make or break your look. The best lighting you can have is natural light with just a slight warm undertone. But if you're not lucky enough to shoot during the 'golden hours' of the day or have a window right in front of you, you can fake it. Cue the iPhone clip-on light or LuMee, or, for us in the broadcast world, three-point lighting. The point is proper lighting can smooth out lines on your face, erase unwanted shadows and create a focal point (that's you) in a picture or video.

If you walk into a news studio, you'll be sur-prised to see how many big lights are floating above the anchor's heads. Hot, powerful lights that can be your best friend or worst enemy. Like I said, good lighting can smooth you out a bit, but too much light can wash you out.

....

That's why a made-up TV face
is three times as intense as
your everyday makeup.

....

Sure, we may take the same steps when put-ting on makeup, but then we add more and then some more. As in extreme contours, eyeliner and lips to make sure definition reads on the lens. Then there's the actual heat that these lights give off. Nothing is less attractive than a face that's melting off. Thank goodness for waterproof mascara, silicon-based primers and lipliner. They've become a reporter's dear friend.

While we're talking external appearances, I think it's important to note the prevalence of Botox and fillers within my industry. Shoot, within any industry. I don't get why these topics are so taboo. Maybe some people consider this plastic surgery and thus fake, but hey I don't. There's not a silicon something living within my body. These tweaks are temporary (although I wish they weren't) and your body naturally metabolizes them. Also, WHO CARES if you have had plastic surgery. I'm sorry, why is plastic surgery deemed fake while your gel nails and bottled blonde hair isn't? I mean, even mascara isn't natural. Am I right? I'm dyeing my eyelashes every day to create a different appearance. I'm just saying everyone has a line. Don't judge me for mine and I won't judge you for yours.

Meghan Anne Bunchman

....

Why are beauty and brains mutually
exclusive? Can't I be educated
and also care about how I look?

....

With that said, Botox and fillers are a very real thing within my business. Why? Perhaps it's because we spend anywhere between one to four hours on TV each day. Typically, that times out to be about 88 minutes of facetime. No, not the app, but full on close-ups of just you and your face for the world to see. We and our viewers (lucky us) are dissecting every detail of our face. From our unruly brows, to paper-thin lips, to those little creases on our foreheads where makeup tends to settle. I'm just saying that if part of your job was to study yourself on camera and virtually analyze all the good and bad parts of yourself 24/7, you'd probably find some flaws too.

It's like when you're in a hotel bathroom and decide to use that 10x mirror to put on your makeup. Ahhh ... just kidding. Abort that mission. That's way too close. My bruised ego prefers dimmed lights and perhaps blurry vision. I'm a Monet. What can I say? Anyways, for me I have used Botox to specifically target a wrinkle above my left eyebrow. I don't go often, but probably twice a year I put a couple of units in my forehead to make sure my cakeup (that's caked on makeup) goes on smoothly and settles well.

I've tried filler before within my lips. Ever since I was a little girl I've been lusting after plumper lips. In fact, if I did the math, I bet I'd find that I've spent thousands of dollars in my lifetime trying to plump up my peckers. Sadly though, no lip venom has ever lived up to its name. So, at the age of 28 I decided it was time to try Juvederm. This filler or injectable is expensive. (I'm not going to lie.) Especially for a news anchor who doesn't make as much as you'd think. A full syringe, which can be stored in a medical fridge for up to a year of use, typically retails between 600 to 800 dollars. But hey, I had exhausted all other avenues and was desperate. With that said, I liked the results. I really did! I finally had plump lips that kept their shape when I smiled. The only problem: my body metabolized the injectable incredibly fast. I'm talking within two months my lips were back to normal. (Sometimes life isn't fair.) And my frugal self wasn't going to keep paying for such a short, temporary result. In the end, I returned to my trustee lip liner. I now just overline the crap out of my lips and work hard to create the illusion that they're natural. Remember, smoke and mirrors?

I won't name names, but I know dozens of female news anchors and reporters who have had "work done." From boob jobs to nose jobs to quick eyelid lifts, we're all doing it. But it's not just us in the TV world. We, as women, are all doing it. Perhaps if we started being more open about the little tweaks we're making, the idea of fillers and plastic surgery wouldn't be so shunned. I'm all for respecting your right for privacy. You do you. But when someone blatantly lies about not having "work done" when asked, they are perpetuating an unrealistic and unhealthy standard for the next generation.

Some of my favorite tools...

Anastasia Brow Stencils

I'm a fan of anything that you can't screw up no matter how hard you try. Seriously, these little babies are like paint by numbers for your face. Step one: identify your brow shape and arch height. Step two: align the stencil with your brow. Step three: color within the lines. Voila, perfect

Kardashian like brows even for us pale-skinned beauties.

Lip Cheat Pillow Talk

Remember how I said I've always wanted plump lips, but after trial and error realized Juvederm was way too expensive for such short-term results? Or, that I've spent thousands of dollars trying every venom, bite and plumper out there only to burn my skin and spend the next week caking on concealer? Well, like any good science experiment, after changing the variable hundreds of times, I've finally figured out how to achieve the perfect pout: pillow talk. Charlotte Tilbury's lip cheat pencil in color "pillow talk" will change your life. The color is so perfect that you can line, outline and then outline that outline of your lips and still look natural. The only catch is, this liner is a little on the pricey side. But trust me, that $22 is money well spent.

Morphe Eyeshadow Palettes

Want to talk about bang for your buck? Look no further than Morphe. I discovered this product during one of my deep dives into Jaclyn Hill's makeup tutorials (hey, girl hey). For a while the palettes were available only online, but in a recent shopping trip I noticed Sephora is now stocking them. The prices IMHO are incredibly reasonable. Palettes consisting of 35 different colors, ranging from $25 to $40. Plus, the actual pigment and texture of the shadows are unmatched. Creamy and saturated, these palettes beat out designer products that are triple the price.

Estee Laudre Double Wear

Days can be long in the news world. I'd like to tell you that every day is predictable, controlled and pleasant, but I was raised Catholic, so I know better than to lie. What may have started out to be a fun, live shot, covering a new brewery that doubles as a bowling alley, can quickly turn into an active shooter shutting down a major freeway. No, the bowlers didn't snap off, but breaking news did. So, my three hours of planned fun quickly pivots to 10 hours of wall-to-wall coverage outside in the elements. Thus, my face makeup better be long wearing (and I mean long wearing). Estee Lauder's Double Wear is full coverage and so long-lasting that even the Florida heat won't melt it away.

iPhone Ring Light

Lighting can make or break any picture and video. If you are committed to the art of the perfect selfie or perhaps a travel vlogger, you'll set

your alarm for that 4 a.m. wakeup call to capture images during sunrise (the golden hour).
Long shadows, warm light and quiet surround-
ings make for the perfect shot. But if you're not a
morning person, there are ways to fake that natural glow: a ring light. Most of these lights clip
on to your phone or computer easily, and have
different levels and tones of brightness.

Meghan Anne Bunchman

Helmet Head Is
Never A Good Look

"You've got that TV hair"

A COUPLE OF YEARS AGO I WAS bullied and basically forced to chop and dye my natural, blonde locks to a dishwater-brown bob for work. Don't believe me... just ask my hair stylist and the several other co-workers who were told (or intimidated) to do the same. Here's the thing, a national magazine published a digital piece in the not so recent past about the "Anchor haircut." Truthfully, there is a TV haircut that tends to look good on most women for on-air purposes. The kicker though, someone I previously worked with was quoted as saying she's never been told how to rock her hair. She is gorgeous and sweet, and I'm sure she was speaking her truth. But for a quote like that to run as if it represented the majority of my then-workplace is misleading.

Back to the story: my natural blonde was being washed out by the light, so I was "strong handed" to dye it. I did. And I hated it! Honesty! It was not a flattering color for me, and, over time I let my natural color blend back in. This may sound vain on some level, but I'm sure you can relate to this, even if we're not talking hair. How about a moment in your workplace that you felt like you had to 'comply' with the corporate request or face internal backlash, or, even worse … dismissal.

....

The lesson I learned from this experience: trust your gut or at the very least have them pay for it!

....

I'm not here for a rant or to be a victim with a swan song. That's not the point. I'm here to tell you there is yet another standard that female anchors are asked to live up to when it comes to hair. A mid-length bob that is styled straight is preferred along the East Coast and in the Midwest, while a bit sexier curls and length is acceptable on the west side of our country. Why? Because people on the east side of the nation like a more serious, business like appearance. While on the West Coast TV news is another form of entertainment.

There has been an even bigger shift lately in hiring the right look without previous experience. Welcome to the new world of "TV first and then the news." ... Dare I say TV news anchors have now shifted to TV news actors?

No matter which style you see, you can bet a teasing comb is somewhere to be found in that green room. From filling out some thinning hair to adding some height and definition to your scalp, a teased head ensures a great look. Then there's our not-so-secret weapon: hair spray. Honestly, I bet I go through a can of hair spray every three weeks. Helmet head (in the most natural way) is a must, especially if you're reporting outside in the elements. I personally am a fan of Velcro rollers. Yes, like those 80s neon dollar store finds that bring body to your mane. A bonus for those working the morning shift and stumbling into the newsroom at 3 a.m. I mean, if I'm up at that hour, I at least want to give producers something to talk about.

The key to any given anchor haircut, in the end, is consistency. In the ideal world, a reporter's hair and makeup look should be the same every single day. I'm not saying that we won't switch to a more fall shade of lipstick once the season changes, but wearing your hair up one day and curly the next doesn't create a consistent brand.

....

And, in the end, whatever field you work in, your outward appearance represents your brand.

....

In case you didn't know, hair extensions are a very real thing within my industry. From adding thickness, length or just texture, extensions and wigs have become just part of our daily routine. Most women I know who use them prefer clip-ins or the Halo. For the most part, we are just looking to add some fullness to our style. There's also something nice about styling your extensions once and then wearing them for a week or two without having to re-touch them.

As for my dear friends with ethnic hair, the good news for them is that within the past couple of years there's been a wave of going au natural, rocking their beautiful curls and wave that nature intended. But, without speaking out of turn, all of the standards and expectations placed on female anchors and reporters for their on-air appearance is only heightened for non-Caucasian talent.

....

Derogatory stereotypes still
exist within the TV world

....

Sadly, derogatory stereotypes still exist within the TV world, actually within the entire world itself, and, from my observation, ethnic reporters get the short end of the stick. Wigs, extensions and hundreds of dollars spent wasted on straightening their hair just to please and adhere to the expectations of others.

InStyler Blowout Revolving Styler

I'd love to live in a world where weekly blowouts fit within my budget, or schedule for that matter. But between juggling three jobs, two kids and a husband, finding time to shave my legs is a feat. So how do I achieve that consistent blowout look by myself? This InStyler wand is my secret weapon. My crazy, curly hair isn't always the most manageable, but this tool has changed my hair game. Don't judge me, but here's another confession: I wash my hair only once a week. So, after a quick blow dry, I take 15 minutes or so to run this spiraling flatiron through my hair. Smooth, shiny hair in 20 minutes or less.

Halo

When it comes to hair, you get what you pay for. I'm not talking about styling products. I'm talking about buying the hair itself. Fake hair. Extensions. Wigs. Whatever you want to call it. Sure, you can find some fun temporary pieces at your local beauty salon or party store. But if you're trying to pass these extensions off as your natural hair … look at these pieces as an invest-ment. I personally have never used a Halo. For my wedding though, I committed to Bellami tape-ins. Committed is the operative word, be-cause every six weeks you have to go in and get them moved up. Definitely a time commitment. Plus, Bellami hair is very high quality, and you'll pay a premium for them. Thus, a lot of my friends use Halos. High quality, nonsynthetic hair that they can pop on and off themselves in a matter of minutes.

Kevin Murphy Dry Shampoo

If you haven't jumped on the dry shampoo train by now, then I'm not sure we can be friends.

Meghan Anne Bunchman

Seriously. Washing your hair everyday isn't just time consuming, it's actually bad for you. That's right, studies have shown it's actually bad for your scalp. Natural oils are healthy. But an oily look ... I'll pass. Cue dry shampoo (or if you're lucky enough to be as blonde as me, baby powder works too). The best part about the Kevin Murphy product is the smell. It's literally zen in a bottle. Plus, the product builds well and in my experience prolongs your style.

L'Oreal Elnett Satin Hairspry

Remember when I said hairspray is an anchor's best friend? Well meet my BFF L'Oreal. She's a beauty. With a golden body and strong hold, my girl is the best. No, but for real, as a former ballerina now turned news anchor, I've tried just about every hairspray on the market. It's a thin line to walk when it comes to hairspray, because you want a product that is strong enough to withstand straight-line winds (I'm not exaggerating) without giving you the appearance of helmet head. This spray brushes out well and doesn't leave you with that sticky residue.

Words Matter

"Did you really mean to say that?"

LABELS, LANGUAGE, WORDS … whatever you want to call them … they matter. Both from a legal perspective and from a relatability standpoint.

From day one journalists are taught to use specific words or phrases to protect themselves from slander or libel. For example, if a person hasn't been convicted of a crime, they are still a "suspect" or "alleged killer." Or perhaps police are searching for a group of kids they say have been spray painting parks … well, in the news world you'd better say police are looking for three teens "connected to" vandalism in Bluffington area parks. Why?

Broadcast YOUR Beauty

....

Because true journalism
reflects the notion of
"innocent until proven guilty."

....

Then there are words NOT to use when it comes to delivering the news: residents, blaze, spokesperson, altercation, etc. Why? Because those words are so jargony (yep, that's my new word) or impersonal. I mean ... do you identify as a resident of Chicago? Or do you call yourself a local? How about that blaze in your fireplace on a cold winter's night? Not a thing? Mmmhmm, that's called a fire. Did your kids get into an altercation at school? Nope! They got into a fight. Get it? The thing is if you watch your local news, you'll probably still hear TV journalists using some of these antiquated words, but I am telling you now that they are amateurs. Yes, even if they've been with that specific station for decades. Because the point of TV news is to connect with the viewers on a personal level and tell them a story - like two friends chatting over lunch.

Meghan Anne Bunchman

....

Journalists are not meant
to be stenographers.

....

Words can make or break you. Own your words. Own your worth. Stop marginalizing yourself.

....

Our delivery shouldn't be dry,
but personal and with emotion.

....

Now that we've addressed the news world, let's apply those lessons to your daily life. Who are you? Isn't it funny that one of the first questions people ask when meeting each other is "What do you do?" The sad truth is we, as Americans, place a lot of our value in what we do. That's great, if you truly love your job. That's awesome if your job is your calling or vocation. But for the majority of people in the workplace, we somehow stumbled into the career we have. Sure, we may have fun at work and like the structure, but, in its rawest form, our job is simply a paycheck. It's not truly fulfilling. So, I would argue that the question "what do you do," should be replaced by "who are you?" or at the very least superseded.

Who Are You?

Before you answer that question, here are some tips: be definitive, confident and succinct. Broadcast 101 teaches young journalists to write one thought per sentence. This creates simple, declarative sentences that anyone can understand. Journalists are also taught to assume our audience has a 3rd-grade reading level. So keep it simple silly (KISS).

I am a media entrepreneur. I'm a TV and radio News Anchor. I am a News Director. I'm a podcaster. I'm an Adjunct College Professor in - you guessed it - Communications and Media studies. In addition to my job titles, I am a wife. I am a mother of two. I'm a sister, a daughter and an all-around life cheerleader. I am a follower of Jesus. I am a retired dancer. I am a long-distance runner.

Meghan Anne Bunchman

And I could go on and on about things that define me far more than my resume. So ... who are you? Take a moment and answer this question. Seriously. Then look at the phrases you wrote down and simplify them.

Are you just a stay at home Mom? No not JUST... you are a Mom. Are you an assistant to an executive in the music industry that does x, y and z. No, you're an Executive Assistant for a top music producer. Are you a college student whose major is still undecided? No. You're earning your bachelor's degree at an accredited university. When you speak with confidence and in short, succinct sentences ... you'll exude confidence.

....

The sad truth is we, as women, have been taught to not own our successes.

....

I'm not sure when or where that lesson happened, but somewhere down the line little girls were slowly molded to put everyone else's desires, wishes and accomplishments before themselves. We deflect when the attention is on us. We become self-deprecating when a compliment comes our way. We defuse with "I'm sorry" to change subjects. Oh, and we add "just" to just about every typed email or request that comes our way. Example: I just wanted to follow-up with you or I just wanted to see how the assignment is going. NO. No more just! I wanted to follow-up with you. How's the assignment going?

Stop reducing your worth through words.

Own your worth. Own your truth. Own your power. Own your words.

Time to practice what I preach (and teach!) For most of us it's not going to be easy to own our power at first. You'll probably stumble and mumble your way through the first couple of rounds. But guess what?

....

Practice makes permanent.
So, start freaking practicing!

....

Pull up that last email you sent to your boss or co-worker. Now take a good long look. Analyze it. Edit it down. Did you apologize for something you didn't even do? Why? I mean, if you didn't cause pain, discomfort or whatever hiccup happened in the workplace why are YOU saying sorry. Stop that immediately! Seriously. Now look for the word just in your messaging. Did you find it? How many times did you repeat that word within a simple "checking in" email? Now acknowledge it and then cut it out (literally and figuratively in your next email). Don't default to phrases or words that marginalize your voice.

....

Remember: simple declarative
sentences demand attention.

....

1. Time to write down how you identify your workself. What do you do? Don't marginalize that answer to make someone else comfortable. Own your value. Own it, say it and practice it in the mirror. You know how companies create their one-minute "elevator pitch ..." well, I'm challenging you to take that same idea and create an elevator pitch about yourself.

Do it. Do it now. I'll wait ...

Delivery

"You nailed that speech!"

I'M SURE BY NOW YOU'VE HEARD that public speaking is the number one fear of people worldwide. Number one, really? I mean, what about being attacked by a shark or getting cancer or being chased by dinosaurs, because you know *Jurassic Park* could actually happen? Just me? In all seriousness though, stage fright and speaking to a crowd of four or 4,000 seems to be the great equalizer. I mean, whether you're the CEO of a multimillion-dollar company or an intern in college, presenting is scary and humbling.

....

The fear of public speaking
is the great equalizer.

....

Broadcast YOUR Beauty

I'm just going to rip the Band-Aid off right at the beginning of this chapter and tell you the only way you can get over this fear is by facing it head on … again and again. Until one day you have enough reps under your belt that the idea of fear doesn't even enter your mind. With that said, there are plenty of tips and tricks you can do to set yourself up for that home run of a speech.

Preparation is everything. Believe me. As someone who has done thousands of live shots (reporter jargon for live reporting) you can't fake what you don't know. Sure, if it's an interview you can focus on asking open-ended questions and let your interviewee fill-in the rest. But what happens if you're previewing a political rally at your local arena that night? Well, if I don't do my research I (the anchor or reporter) could be spewing off #fakenews. I mean, we wouldn't want that to happen, right? "The rally starts at 9 p.m." (or 6 p.m. if I had read the press report) and "is open to the public" (or not - because according to the release, tickets are required). Don't look like a fool. Do your homework.

Once you've researched what you want to talk about, it's time to edit. Edit down your thoughts. The best advice I can give here is to make one point per sentence. Don't confuse your listeners with irrelevant details and anecdotes. Make your point fast. Be succinct. Drop all jargon. Be relatable. Sounds easy, right? Well go ahead and review your notes for that upcoming presentation, or even job interview, and see if that's how you wrote it. If not, edit away.

Only after your point has been made can you go into that pre-rehearsed story about why that point was so necessary in a fill-in-the-blank situation. One thought per sentence and breath. Say it with me: breathe. Deep breath in, and exhale out. Relax. Seriously, don't rush through your presentation. Focus on being present. Best tip here is to take a breath every time you come to that metaphorical punctuation.

One thought per sentence, breathe and now curate your supporting material and facts. I like the idea of making a point in threes. Not three points in one sentence. But the same point, three times over. I'm not sure if there is some psychological theory behind giving three examples or supporting factors, but in my experience, people start hearing what you're saying only after that third mention. I tend to go a step further and like to highlight my three supporting factors by holding up corresponding fingers as well. Nonverbal cues should support your speech. But hey, I'm a hand talker so there's that.

Broadcast YOUR Beauty

....

Handgina. You're never going
to forgive me for this one.

....

The next time you watch your local news or a
speaker on stage notice their hands. If that person
is nervous or over thinking their body language,
you'll start seeing their hands forming a diamond
shape over their nether regions. Thus, creating
the handgina. You're welcome.

Pockets are your friend when giving a speech
while standing. Go ahead and put one hand in
your pocket. Look at that, you automatically look
cool and relaxed. The subtle change brings a note
of confidence to your demeanor. Better yet, step
away from that podium and start walking and talking with your hands. I'm not sure about you, but
I am an avid hand gesture speaker. Specifically,
when I'm trying to make a very sensitive point.
Just ask my husband or kids when I'm upset. I
like to make points in threes and thus, you better
believe you'll find me holding up one finger for
each point. Why?

Meghan Anne Bunchman

....

Because body language should,
at the very least, echo your words
if not enhance your voice.

....

Just be careful and don't fall prey to the handgina stature when you stop walking. Ahhh. Embarrassing.

Delivery is so much more than speaking. Delivery is body language. Telling a story rather than just reading words. Emoting sadness in your face when you're covering a school shooting. Smiling when those ducklings are finally rescued from a drain by your local fire department. Emotionally connecting and emphasizing impactful moments through your tone and facial expression rather than reading scripts monotonically.

Apart from your hands, your eyes and mouth can show emotion for better or for worse. I'll admit it, on days that I'm just reading the news instead of connecting with it, my eyes look dead on camera. There's no warmth or emotion behind them. I'm not engaged and even if I deliver a flawless newscast my eyes give it away. One of my dear friends actually taught me this after months of studying my own delivery on camera. She taught me to Smize. Yes, Tyra Banks style. Smile with your eyes. Emote with your eyes. Let the viewers see someone's at home in that big, beautiful brain of yours.

Smizing may not come natural to you at first. So, you'll have to force it. Force that smile both physically with your mouth and warmth with your eyes. Notice how people start responding to you. No, you're not being fake. You're building a new muscle of connecting to your words. Let's test it out: the next time you're on the phone (even if it's with a telemarketer) smile through the entire call. I bet you if you do, you'll find whomever is on the other end more attentive and helpful. Now flip that experiment around and start listening to the person on the other end. Are they smiling? This may sound crazy, but if you exercise this muscle and new tip enough, you'll actually be able to hear if that person is smiling on the other end of the line. Now take that trick with you, and good luck on your next phone interview.

....

Delivery has a lot to do with listening.

....

58

Meghan Anne Bunchman

Finally, I think it's important to note that delivery also has a lot to do with listening. Picture this: a reporter on scene of a horrific fire that engulfed a senior living facility. Well, according to officials everyone got out safely. But as the reporter interviews an elderly woman, she mentions that her husband, a retired Marine, ran back into the building to get their friend Sam out. Well, Sam is now standing by this woman's side, but where is her husband? Listen to her and then follow-up! If a reporter is so busy thinking of his or her next question, they may miss the actual story. This retired Marine is missing, and firefighters don't know he went back in the building.

....

Listen to understand, not to respond.

....

That's why I like to tell people to listen. The easiest way to master this trick is purely by being present. I know, I know that doesn't seem hard. But how many times have you found yourself driving to work and then halfway there you realized you don't remember the first half of that drive at all? Again, as someone who spent years rolling into a newsroom at 3 a.m., I can tell you that weird phenomenon was more like a monthly experience for me. So be present and listen. This is particularly helpful when you're in a fight with a loved one or friend. If you're so focused on firing back and getting that zinger in, you'll miss the point of his or her grievance entirely. How about when you're pitching a product to a new business? Well, if they tell you their clients don't have access to the internet, then you'd better come up with a solution rather than rattling off more facts about your great new app.

How to deliver a killer speech.

1. Research. Know what you're talking about. Know what the opposition says. Know what the next frontier is. It's always better to be over prepared, so you don't find yourself ad libbing to a fault. (As in having to retract statements later on because you didn't know enough in the first place.)

2. Practice. Get enough reps under your belt that you're no longer thinking about what is next. By practicing, you'll shake out any flaws and start exercising your competency muscle. Remember: practice makes permanent. So don't allow yourself to stumble through a practice round. Stop, breath and re-do it.

3. Edit. People tend to say too much. I'd rather listen to a poignant five-minute *Ted Talk* than an hour-long college lecture. People have a short attention span (especially in today's social media world) so use that knowledge to your advantage. Cut out unnecessary words, anecdotes and redundancies. Remember: one thought per sentence.

4. Breath. As in breath at the end of each sentence. Breath when you come to a theoretical comma, colon or period. So many people rush through their speeches. If you race through your presentation, your points will probably not be heard. Allow for that negative space. (A moment of silence allows your points to really resonate.)

5. Find your power stance. Step away from that podium and start walking. Don't fall into the trap of the dreaded handgina. Use your hands to enhance your story.

Know Your Audience

"You talking to me? You talking to me..."

DON'T BE OFFENDED, BUT news writers are told to write as if they're speaking to someone with a third-grade reading level. That's not meant to be mean; it's meant to be inclusive. Although each station has "its person" (more on that later) the news is meant to capture the attention of the masses by casting a wide net.

Don't waste time bloviating or spatting off SAT words – news anchors shouldn't be concerned with proving their smarts, and you shouldn't either for that matter. Instead, they should be striving toward relatability.

Speaking of a station's "person," ask any reporter and they'll be able to show you a physical description and demographic breakdown of their station's Joe Schmoe or Sally Sue (also known as their key viewer). Why is this important to know? Well, if you know who your person is, then you know what they're interested in. In parts of the Midwest, it's not uncommon for your person to be most interested in agriculture, breweries and hockey. That understanding of their likes then dictates how a producer stacks a newscast. Perhaps that ribbon-cutting ceremony about a new trendy boutique doesn't merit a lead spot in the newscast.

....

What makes a story newsworthy
typically has to
do with the impact.

....

Some markets stick to the old adage: "if it bleeds, it leads." But for the most part that way of thinking has become outdated. I'm not saying the audience won't show empathy to the mother who lost her son in a car crash, but in reality, the "newsworthiness" of this story may directly impact only four people. Now, if the crash shut down traffic on a major freeway for hours, it's likely more people were impacted; thus, the story may be bumped up to the beginning of the newscast.

The same way of thinking can be applied to the next speech you give, or business presentation or even an awkward cocktail hour with complete strangers. I mean, you're not going to talk about your favorite moscow mule drink in a room full of alcoholics, right? How about giving a Pantone color presentation to a room of visually impaired? No, that would be inappropriate and in poor taste. Thus, knowing who you are talking to and their values are key!

....

A person's why is far more
important and telling than their what.

....

So, who is your audience? This answer will be complicated, multifaceted and far more than just a job title. Why? Because people are complicated. Why? Because people relate to stories not facts. Why? Because people connect with emotion not statistics. Sure, you're going in to interview for a marketing assistant job and you've done your research on the company. But have you done your research on the person who is actually interviewing you?

I'd like to assume that of the five people being interviewed for the job all of them will have that perfectly typed resume and rehearsed go-to answers. So what else are you going to do or say to stand out? Does your interviewee run marathons? Well then it might be smart to casually mention that you're training for the local 5k coming up. (That is, if you actually are.) How about that company being a nonprofit organization? Well, it may be smart to mention the outside volunteering you do at your local kennel. If you know what others are interested in, you can use that information to be more impactful.

So, here's how detailed a TV station's "person" profile gets:

Meet Harry. He's a 46-year-old father of two. His wife, Jane, works as a school teacher in their district. Harry is a white man with a bachelor's degree from the University of Wisconsin. He works at Iron Construction Works as a mid-level manager and earns close to $80,000 annually. Harry graduated from Appleton High School in 1991 and now lives just down the street. When he's not at work, Harry spends his weekends along the lakeshore fishing with his sons. He loves the brands Columbia, Apple and Orvis. Oh, and a weekend Starbucks run has become a family tradition for Harry. Every Sunday Harry and his family go to church and then he coaches his boy's soccer team at the local YMCA. He enjoys watching ESPN, Netflix, BTN and XYZ TV. He typically spends about two hours on Facebook and LinkedIn per day. Harry's wife shops at Costco, Kroger, Macy's and Home Depot. They drive a Jeep Grand Cherokee and a Yukon. Harry voted for President Trump and likes to listen to Rush Limbaugh. Harry's biggest concern during the last national election was the economy.

By the way, political campaigns create a similar profile. By identifying common traits their voters share, those campaigns know which pond to fish in for a greater turnout. The Prius pond for liberal candidates or the Meat and Potato pond for conservative hopefuls. Yes, those are just stereotypes. Please don't get offended! It's just an example.

Now it's time to identify your audience.

1. Name your person (aka your product consumer). Who are they? Where did they grow up? What are their beliefs?

2. What does your person do, and, more importantly, what motivates your person to go to work? Money, maybe. Passion, possibly. Structure, perhaps.

In this case, the why is greater than the what. So think, reflect and write it down.

3. What does he/she do for fun? Are they a foodie or beer lover? How about an avid bowler? Do they compete in Iron Mans?

Remember people are multi-faceted and their job title is only one part of whom they are.

Meghan Anne Bunchman

Uniquely You

"We don't need another blonde"

THIS IS GOING TO BE A CONtroversial thing to say given the current climate of racial equality within the United States, but being a white, blonde female in the news world puts you at one of the greatest disadvantages. Why? Because blondes are a dime a dozen - or at least that's what one News Director once told me. Why? Because "blonde bombshells" can't possibly know sports - or at least that's what several viewers have so sweetly written to me about. Why? "Because blondes are meant to be seen and not heard" - a former boss once said to me. Thank you for that.

Broadcast YOUR Beauty

....

Your local news team is
supposed to reflect the
demographic of where you live.

....

As in, if you're turning on the morning news
in Houston, you'll find more Spanish speaking
reporters. Or if you live in an urban city, you'll
likely see more black reporters on TV. How
about LA? Time to roll out your Jessica Rabbits
and Rico Suave's of the world. Now this may all
sound well and good - and maybe even fair - at
first glance, but how would you feel if I told you
those "demographically pleasing reporters" may
have no experience or even media training, yet
they're here to bring you the truth through research and facts. True, you can learn quickly on
the job, especially in this field, but nothing will
ever trump good, old fashioned repetition.

....

There's a shift toward news
actors nowadays ... experience and
education have gone by the wayside.
Entertainment trumps news.

....

Meghan Anne Bunchman

In the ideal world (or at least mine) the hiring process would be solely based on a meritocracy - like sports. The man or woman with the most experience and best game would be hired. Period. But that's not reality.

Thus, circling back to the chapter's lead … I am NOT just another blonde. I could sit here and shout from a soap box "take me seriously," but honestly it would fall upon deaf ears. So, what can I do? No, I'm not going to dye my hair - been there, regret that. No, I'm not going to wear lower-cut dresses. No, I'm not going to take "you're just another blonde" as the final word. Damn right I'm a blonde! But I'm also a seasoned reporter with 10 years of experience. A reporter who's covered national news from the White House and the Hill. A reporter who's experienced boot camp alongside United States Marines down in Parris Island, SC. An anchor with a master's degree from Northwestern University. An anchor who has interviewed a half dozen presidential candidates. So no, I am not just another blonde. I am me. And that's enough!

Time to do some work.

What makes you stand out? By the way, I'm not just talking about how you stand out in the workforce. Sure, rattling off some statistics to show the efficiency of your new algorithm is great, but even if you're the smartest in the room, people connect with your story not your stats.

Be vulnerable, open up a bit. You don't have to share your entire personal life with Sally on the third floor, but a bit of what you do for fun won't hurt. Also, take this from me and a lesson I learned early on in my career: if you're an asshole, people won't want to work with you.

....

Newsflash: Kindness trumps statistics ... always.

....

So, what makes you unique? Are you a marathoner? Great! That shows me your dedication and long-term commitment to a goal. What about an avid home organizer? Awesome. That tells me you are meticulous and have impeccable attention for details. Do you volunteer? Well I love to see people with a philanthropic mindset. They're gracious and intentional with their time.

That unique perspective, creativity and voice can be seen played out on TV news channels every day. Ever notice that the top three stories of each newscast on all of your local TV stations tend to be the same? As in that shooting in South Side, Chicago, a major downtown construction project and a weekend presidential visit all appear on your local CBS, ABC, FOX and NBC affiliates, but perhaps in a different order. Why? Well, first because those are the most newsworthy stories. But why are the stories arranged differently? That's easy too: each TV station's audience is a little different. One station may have a more politically minded demographic, while another's key demo is perhaps those living in downtown Chicago near that construction project. But in the end, those three stories kick off your chosen nightly newscast. So, what makes coverage on one of the stories more interesting or compelling than the other? You (or technically the reporter). Their voice. Their shooting style. (That's videography.) Their delivery. Their storytelling.

....

Remember, facts tell ... stories sell.

....

Think about it. If all three news stations have the same facts - the who, what, wheres of a story

- what makes one story's coverage more compelling? I mean, they all have the same statistics. They all have the same official interviews with law enforcement. They all have similar camera shots of the crime scene. So why does a viewer prefer one station's news package (pre-produced story) over another's? Cue that emotional connection. Emotions create that human factor that stats will never be able to provide. Sure, the facts may show this is the 13th homicide of the year. But the emotion, that mother crippled over in pain, because her 5-year-old daughter was an innocent victim of crossfire … that is the image and sound that will stay with you long after the story airs.

Human emotion matters.
Intimacy matters.
Your uniqueness matters.

Meghan Anne Bunchman

Years on the job ≠ Experience

"You don't know what you're talking about"

WITHIN THE PAST DECADE the TV news world has changed dramatically. Blame it on the recession or greedy big businesses or whatever ... even still gone are the days of the reporter, videographer (we call them photogs) and field producer dedicated to just one story. Now you'll typically see a reporter in full makeup (men too) and heels (not men) slinging 50 pounds worth of camera equipment and a tripod over his or her shoulder as they walk a mile through a crowd of protesters just to find the best visual. Seems dramatic or hyperbolic? Nope. It's a daily hike for many of us.

MMJs – Multimedia Journalists

Anyways, these new reporters are most commonly known as MMJs or multimedia journalists. What does that mean exactly? Basically, this individual is doing the total of three jobs for a fifth of the cost. As in the MMJ is shooting their own story, editing it and then live tossing to it (fronting the pre-produced story) all out of the back seat of his or her car. In truth, the quality of the storytelling greatly diminishes, because these MMJanes (in my case) now have to factor in drive time, shoot time, interviews and editing within their already tight deadlines. But from a business perspective, cutting jobs is great for its bottom line: money. I mean, you can be a jack of all trades but a master of none, you know?

But I digress. Now that's what's expected for newcomers into the field, but what about those "staples" within your market who have been behind the desk for decades?

The staples – behind the desk for decades

In my experience, many of those so-called staples are so caught up in the old way of thinking - the "I've paid my dues" - that their skills have become sloppy or even worse: antiquated. Maybe they have put in the work, maybe they haven't. That's not for me to say. But guess what: news is different now and these "MMJs" with five years of experience under their belt typically outweigh and outperform that "staple" who hasn't left the newsroom since Clinton was in office.

Am I sounding hypocritical? Yes! Here I am talking about the trials of being an MMJ and the reduction of quality news while criticizing the old ways of the news world and its "staples." It's true that news quality has greatly decreased since the rise of the MMJ. That's also in part because the number of people within a newsroom has greatly decreased.

....

There are less eyes on a story
to fact check, edit and filter ideas through.

....

But there has also been a new renaissance to storytelling since MMJs came on scene. Why? Because we have less time and still the same amount of pride; thus, creativity prospers. It's the old adage of working smarter not harder. As in shooting a story with multiple cameras, silly stand-ups (that's when the reporter pops in front

81

of the camera during the produced package to bridge a thought or transition) and viral sound-bites.

Now back to those "staples" who have been bringing you the "latest news" for decades. Decades is the operative word here. As in decades of not evolving. Decades of not updating their skills. Decades of refusing to learn about new technology and the ins and outs of every job within the newsroom (in any career really). Not because they have to, but because they want to. I think we can all agree that when you live a day in someone else's shoes you'll, at the very least, appreciate all they do. Also, those "staples" are still speaking in their version of a "Walter Cronkite" voice. Why. Do. We. Have. To. Talk. In. Such. A. Weird. Cadence. Thank you … and goodnight.

And what about the GOATS

Now I want to give a shout out to those GOATs who have been in the news world for decades and continue to evolve. They never let ego get in their way, and they've embraced the new news world. That is awesome. You are awesome. And … you are rare. Thank you!

Without saying names, one of the newsrooms I used to work in had a culture of "failing upwards." Yes, a new term my then co-workers and I coined about those who had been working in said newsroom for twenty years, achieved executive-level jobs, and, for the life of them, couldn't write a 20-second news story to save their lives. Hence: they failed up. These people tended to be a lot of yes-(wo)men or pawns within the company. They realized (some would argue smartly) by doing what was asked of them, even if it compromised their integrity or ethics, they'd be promoted. With no regard for what was right, or drive to work towards a transparent product that chooses quality over quantity, they blindly followed orders.

Some business people may read this and think, "yeah, that's what you call a good employee." But if I could tell you some of the things that happened or were a consequence of those actions, you'd be appalled. With that said, that's not what this book is about. I'm not here to spat off negativity. I want to build you up, to help you recognize different types of people within the workforce and teach you how to navigate gracefully through moments like these. So, notice them. Acknowledge them. And then play the game, if possible while circumventing them. That's all you can do.

Target acquired: ready, aim, fire

"They won't even see my comment."

SOCIAL MEDIA IS A FUNNY thing. It's the great connector and also the ultimate destroyer. I've been lucky enough to connect and build strong, authentic friendships with people I have never met in person through social media. I've networked. Curated partnerships and even bonded with men and women thousands of miles away from me.

But then there's the flip side: the destructive nature of posts, tweets and #ootds. They say comparison is the thief of happiness, and with the selfie-obsessed world we now live in let me tell you, there are times in my life that my happiness has fallen by the wayside. However, I would argue that comparison can be controlled and not the biggest problem in the world of social media. Comparison is a choice. A muscle you can exercise to avoid feelings of FOMO or jealousy. What, in my opinion, is the scariest reality of social media? It is the lack of intimacy.

Think about it. You don't know the story behind that smile or the struggle behind a triumphant post. You comment or judge purely based on a screen grab or snapshot of someone's life. Social media has created an anonymity for trolls and a platform for hatred.

I'm not saying all social media is bad, but a tool exploited can quickly become a weapon.

Now go with me here - I believe social media, to bullies, is what bombs were, to war, in the 20th century. Whether you believe in war or not, there used to be an intimacy in battle. You could see the eyes of the man or woman you were fighting. You'd see them bleed. You'd see them grieve. You'd see them suffer. But when technology advanced and the ability to drop missiles on troops while flying thousands of feet above became a reality, the extreme pain of war was instantly hidden.

Meghan Anne Bunchman

The same can now be said about social media. I'm not condoning bullying by any means, but there use to be a time when a bully could see - and hopefully reflect on - their actions towards another. Now with just a quick comment, post or tweet, damaging words can be sent, and yet the impact on their intended target goes unseen by the sender. I wonder if someone would say the same thing they tweet or post about you to your face? My guess is they wouldn't, because there is a feeling of 'safety' when sitting behind a computer. I could go on and on about how destructive cyber bullying is and how hypocritical parents are when they're teaching their kids not to bully at school, and yet don't think twice about sending that "constructive" email. But that conversation is for another time.

Now for some real-world advice … don't react … respond. Seriously. It's as simple as that, and yet one of the most difficult lessons to execute. By reacting, you're letting the other person win, because they're getting a primal or emotionally charged rise out of you. By not reacting or responding at all, you're also letting that person win by not calling them out for their horrid behavior. So how do you respond to a person who has confronted you with hatred or judgement? That's easy: with humor and humility.

I was once called a "dumpster baby" on twitter. I'm not sure where this colorful phrase even came from, because I was doing a story on Clinton vs. Trump during the presidential race. But aside from the creative language, the viewer's misguided anger was taken out on me. If this was the first time this viewer tweeted something negative about me, my body or my look, I may have let it slide. But in this case, the viewer had established a disgusting behavior of attacking several anchors within my then-market whenever they reported on a political story that he disagreed with. So, what did I do? Retweet! That's right, if this person feels so empowered to attack someone they've never met, then I'll give them the platform they're looking for so that everyone can see what he had to say. I also added some text in the retweet saying, "I hope your day is as lovely as you are." You better believe this person was not okay with his choice after I shined light on to the situation. He quickly deleted the original post. No, I did not receive an apology, but I'd like to believe he'll think twice before sending out a nasty comment in the future.

Meghan Anne Bunchman

As for humility … we've all experienced a moment of being stretched too thin. In the world of live TV, if your concentration strays even just for a second, you can quickly find yourself looking like a fool for all to see. I hear the comment all the time that my job is easy. I mean all you have to do as a "talking head" is read the news, right? Wrong. I'd say nearly 80 percent of my workday happens off-camera.

From finding news stories, conducting interviews, fact checking, editing packages (minute-long stories), refining scripts and updating information, my job keeps me busy. As for when you're on camera, many newsrooms have switched to the on-air talent controlling the teleprompter. (Because floor directors and even interns became another casualty in the recession.) Typically, it's by a foot pedal or dial under the news desk. Oh, and then there's that little voice in your head shouting out developing stories and which in-studio camera production is about to take. Yes, an actual voice also known as your producer. That is why you'll see anchors wearing little earpieces called IFBs. Sometimes even stereotypically pressing those ear pieces deep into their ears to hear their producer over the sounds of jeers and protests around them.

So yeah, sometimes I do get distracted, and sometimes viewers call me out for it. That's fine. They're right and I'll tell them that. But I also explain that we are all human and sometimes I'm just having an off day or they're not seeing what's going on behind camera. To accept criticism in a gracious manner, while giving insight to details viewers aren't typically privy to, is how I define humility.

I'm not saying you should respond to every post, rude remark said within ear shot or gossip at the water cooler.

....

For me, I believe in responding to patterns, whether that's good patterns of behavior or bad.

....

Because hey, we all have an off day. So how do you apply a TV news problem to your real-world job? The same way.

Meghan Anne Bunchman

Respond, don't react. Reaction is full of ego and hurt feelings, while responding comes from a place of understanding and calculation. By the way, sometimes no response is actually the right response. As in knowing when to walk away. There's a difference between knowing when to quit vs giving up.

Think about that.
Let it marinate in your brain.

Don't be too social

"What do your socials say about you?"

NOW THAT WE'VE ESTABLISHED that a social media presence is necessary in the modern world to boost your online profile and yet creates a virtual target for all those trolls out there, let's talk about why it's important to not be too social.

At one point, Facebook was the next best thing - even cool for us millennials. I mean, at one point you couldn't even have an account without an Ivy League email or at the very least .edu address. Then it became a platform for the masses. A platform to keep up with family halfway around the world. A platform to let someone know if you were single or not. A platform for marketing. Even a platform to create this almost Sims-like life. "Here's my highlight reel! Now tell me how fabulous I am!" I'm not saying any of this is a bad thing, but it is a relatively new concept for the 21st century.

....

Our anticipated concept of privacy no longer exists within this social media world

....

Sure, in theory we all say we don't want our information out there, but then you're posting a picture of your family while on vacation. Ummm, all robbers out there want to thank you for that empty house notice. How about posting a eulogy for your first dog who you just put down - I mean, he is man's best friend after all. Well guess what, hackers now know the answer to a standard security question. The online world has turned into a popularity contest where posters are always looking for that next like while hackers are looking for the next target. Great in the short term, but buyers be warned: danger ahead.

On-air I go by Meghan Bunchman because - you know - that's my name or at least it was for the first 29 years of my life. Between news opens and standard out cues in story packages, I bet I say my full name close to 20 times a day. I'm used to hearing it. It's my name after all, and it's my TV brand more importantly. But here's the downfall, the only Bunchmans out there are my family. So yes, I have a professional Facebook page for work, but once upon a time my personal profile would pop up on the search engine too.

The line between professional and personal can quickly become blurred in a viewer's mind. In fact the line of professional and personal can quickly get blurred in any work relationship. I learned that the hard way.

....

It is important to establish
appropriate boundaries.

....

It's both a triumph and a curse when you find yourself being so relatable to viewers. On one side, these viewers are inviting me into their living rooms every day while they're in their most vulnerable state - pajamas and coffee in hand. They trust me. They embrace me. They confide in me. While on the flip side, when viewers start thinking they actually know you, they feel empowered to tell you what they're actually thinking. "You're much prettier in person" or "you're thinner in real life." It's like an unintentional back-handed compliment. Bless your heart!

Speaking of blurred lines:

My little sister was once contacted by a super viewer of mine. I'm not saying he was scary, but there were definitely stalker-like qualities. This viewer started friend requesting her again and again, commenting on all of her pictures and let's just say making things feel icky. Well, that was a lesson I learned very quickly and corrected even faster. Read: privacy settings on high for my entire family and voila, I dropped my last name entirely on my own personal account.

I have two kids and a husband whom I believe deserve private lives.

Yet another reason that I still sign off via my maiden name. Ladies (sisters, moms, daughters, whomever you are) listen to me carefully … someone else's privacy is not yours to giveaway. Protect them. Respect them. Listen to them. If

they don't want to be tagged, mentioned or pho-
tographed then don't do it!

....

Someone else's privacy is
not yours to giveaway.

....

Speaking of things to stop doing … stop com-
paring yourself to someone else's Instagram page.

....

News flash: that perfectly curated
life you're stalking isn't real,
and more importantly it isn't
helping your self-worth.

....

You've heard the adage that you're the aver-
age of the five people you spend the most time
with? Well ... now apply that lesson to your social
media use. You are the sum of the accounts you
follow and the content you consume. Is that "in-
fluencer" really helping you with your style, or is

she inadvertently hurting your self-esteem? How about that beautiful fitness model? Is she sharing workout tips with you, or are you finding yourself obsessing over obliques you'll probably never achieve. Not because you can't get into shape, but because that model has a team of nutritionists, coaches and doctors on her side. Got me? I could write a whole other book on Instagram and filter dysmorphia. Specifically, its direct relationship to the rise in unrealistic plastic surgery and depression, but I digress.

Now go ahead and get on board the unfollow train. Choo, choo. All aboard! Get out your phone. I'm serious, get it out. I'm waiting ... Start looking at accounts. If that person or brand isn't educating you, inspiring you or adding joy to your life ... click unfollow! Seem like a daunting task? Well I've found a way to unfollow people in smaller, more manageable chunks. Cue Facebook birthday reminders. These notifications are such an easy way to assess the social "friends" you have and decide if they're worth following or if they're just a number at this point. This isn't meant to be mean. I mean come on, if you can't even pinpoint how you met, the chance that they'll notice your unfollow is minimal. You'll thank me later.

....

Once it's out on the internet
you can't take it back!

....

Finally, it's important to remember that once you put something out on the internet, you can't take it back. Even if you delete or untag that tweet immediately ... in some deep web of the online world a crumb of your past post still exists. So be sure you're comfortable with any and all of the information you are putting out there being public forever. And remember, social media is not your soapbox to stand on. Basically, I'm saying don't be a troll.

....

Social media is a tool, not
a weapon. Don't exploit it.

....

Your social media accounts are your personal resume. Are you really getting blackout drunk every other day? Well your Instagram tells me so. What about that fancy car you keep taking pictures of? I don't want to be the one to break it to you, but you drive a Honda Civic. There's nothing wrong with that car, but that electric blue G-wagon isn't yours. The easiest way to gut-check your posts: ask yourself if you'd be okay with both your Mom and boss seeing them. Look, I'm a girl who loves a good boozy brunch every once in a while, but do I really need to post my champagne escapades every single time?

Who does your social media say you are?

1. Your online presence is the modern day first impression. So it's important to remember that what you post, tweet or snapchat doesn't have a shelf life. Sure you may no longer be that 21-year-old college girl who entered a Spring Break contest, but that photo says otherwise. Think of your Instagram, Snapchat and Twitter as your insta-resume. What do you want it to say about you?

2. You are the sum of the five accounts you follow. Sure, we may follow hundreds of people and brands, but which accounts are you consuming on a daily basis? Remember, if someone or something isn't educating you, making you laugh or challenging you to think outside of the box, you shouldn't be following them. Why be crazy enough to welcome things into your life and mind that produce jealousy or regret? Unfollow those accounts immediately.

3. Social media is a tool, not a weapon. So for the love of humanity don't drink and post. And for that matter don't vent and post either. Instead write those words down on a piece of paper, feel them, acknowledge them and then burn them. Social media should not be your proverbial dumping ground.

Check your ego at the door

"Do you know who I am?"

THERE'S NO JOB TOO SMALL. Say it with me: "there's no job too small." I know, I know I hate cliches too, but damn is this accurate. I'd like to tell you I've never messed up and let my ego get in the way. But as a Catholic school graduate I'm smart enough to know the big guy upstairs isn't down for my lies. My ego has controlled me and failed me multiple times. And I bet you I will fail thousands of times more within my life. But hey, practice makes permanent right? So, I acknowledge it, check myself and then work to change it. Let's break this habit together!

Life finds a way of humbling you

The good news is life finds a way of hum-bling you out with sometimes not so glamorous reality checks. Here's a dirty little secret for you (and I do mean dirty): I know my way around a gas station restroom. Ewww. Yuck. I'm going to gag. Yep, I've had all those visceral reactions and more. One second I'm being praised for my poise and style on-air, the next I'm stumbling into a Shell at 4 a.m. begging the attendant to let me use their employee restroom.

In all seriousness though when you're rolling into a newsroom in the witching hour and news breaks, that 20-minute green room beauty routine of yours goes out the window. Sometimes a re-porter is lucky enough to have a photog with her who's driving, which in theory means you have time to put your face on while en route. But more often than not, reporters are using that time to call sources, listen to scanners and fact check state-ments. So, in between that first and second live hit (journalism jargon for report) you find yourself sprawling out the entire contents of your makeup bag across a gas station countertop. Sexy, right? Again … life finds a way of humbling you.

Don't burn that bridge!

How about when you're in the middle of an interview with your city Mayor and you have to bail out in mid-sentence because news just broke. Don't burn that bridge. Be gracious, explain what's happening and then follow-up with an apology note or email the next day. Don't assume that he or she understands the intricacies of your job. Don't let your ego get in the way and not apologize. Don't make assumptions. Explain that you are the "point woman" for your shift and that sometimes things happen.

....

Assumptions, in every aspect of
our lives, are quicksand for the mind.

....

A destructive assumption many people will fall victim to at some point in their lives is the perception that the front desk staff, administrative assistant or even the parking garage attendant won't make or break their success. Wrong. Wrong, wrong, wrong. Wrong on so many levels. I can't tell you how many times a person, who you may not even recall meeting, will circle back with you in a later stage of your career and – if you were kind to them in the past – will pay that generosity forward. Also, companies talk. If you are rude or snippy to the front-of-house staff, you better believe the person interviewing you for your next job will catch wind of it. So check your ego at the door and just be kind. It's such a simple solution and yet so many of us have been programmed to think otherwise.

I know in a previous chapter I talked about how years on the job don't directly correlate with experience because hey, we all know that person in the office who failed upwards. But there is something to be said about being the dumbest person in the room. I'm not talking ethically compromised or ignorant, but more along the lines of life experiences.

I'll tell you a secret:
I strive to be the dumbest person
in the room, and you should too!

For real though, I'd like to think I'm a smart woman. I earned a master's degree from a prestigious university five years ago or so. I'm an adjunct professor at a local college in Michigan. I read multiple newspapers and reports every day.

Meghan Anne Bunchman

Yes, some of that is because that's what my job demands of me, but a lot of my reading stems from me being perpetually curious.

....

Strive to become perpetually curious!

....

I am smart enough to know that I know very little. I am smart enough to know that I can learn something from anyone. I'm smart enough to know that if I am the smartest person at a party, it's time for me to leave. Why? Because I firmly believe if you're not growing, evolving and pushing your limits then you're dying. Think of it like a shark that stops swimming. A shark has got to swim, am I right? Growth is living. Education is fluid. Intelligence is evolving.

....

Living by its very definition means growth. If you're not growing, you are dying.

....

Your ego is only robbing you of progress.

People tend to rise up (or down) to the level of those whom they surround themselves with. So, do you want to keep learning or are you okay with being the same person you are today ten years from now. I'd like to hope within that 10-year span I add a couple more bruises, scars and lessons to my life log. Don't you?

Takeaways:

1. Assumptions are the quickest way to get yourself into trouble. Do you hear me, if you assume you truly are about to make an ass out of yourself. So stay away from that emotional and tumultuous quicksand. Don't assume ever. I mean ever. Ask curious questions to understand why someone is reacting one way or another. Explain why you need to leave, don't assume your co-worker, interview subject or friend for that matter knows every aspect of your life.

2. If you walk into a room and realize you're the smartest person there, leave. Leave immediately. People inevitably will rise or fall to the occasion at hand. If you don't want to be lumped into a group of known mean girls, leave it. If you want to grouped into a crowd of entrepreneurs, join them. Never be the smartest in the room because if you are the only movement you'll experience is backwards motion. Set yourself up to grow. Set yourself up to live. Set yourself up to succeed.

Working While Woman

"Being strategic is not the same as being

conniving"

NOW THAT WE'VE TOUCHED on everything from beauty tips to confidence hacks, it's important to close with the idea of community. Specifically, how important it is to surround yourself with a positive and evolving group of women.

We all know that water, food, shelter, sleep and air are basic human needs. But from a more emotional or psychological angle, I'd argue community needs to be added to that list.

After all, we all crave acceptance. We all want to find a place where we belong; a place where love is unconditional and judgement-free zones truly exist. A place where we, as women, can boast about our successes without being made to feel like we're bragging. We all crave this idea of a female tribe, but what are you doing to create one?

I'd like to say we are in a new world where women don't see other females as their direct competition. I'd like to believe collaborating with fellow females trumps competing. I'd like to say that is our new reality, but in many cases it is still very much the opposite. Somehow, or at some point within our lives, we were indoctrinated to think that there can only be one female in a power position and, thus, we must do whatever is within our means to come out on top. And I believe it's not entirely our fault.

After all the gender pay gap is still very much part of the workplace. As too is the lack of females within leadership positions at major corporations.

....

We, as women, have been pushing for a seat at the male-dominated industry table for so long that once we get there, we forget to pull up a chair for the next female success story.

....

Meghan Anne Bunchman

In my many years of journalism, I can count on one hand the number of times I've seen a female-only newscast either on a local or national level. Just to clarify, I'm talking news. Not entertainment and not lifestyle shows, but actual news. Your dime a dozen nightly newscasts highlighting crime, city millages and sport scores. But a men-only anchor desks is as common as it comes.

Your career is like playing a game of chess.

One of my girlfriends and I have an inside joke about being coconspirators within our own lives. As in, we look at our careers and the moves we make as if we are playing a game of chess. We know that it may be worth sacrificing a pawn or two early on to win the game overall. We acknowledge that it may play into our own advantages when people dismiss us as "just another pretty face." And yes, we understand that we sometimes have to play the game by someone else's terms to start, but after establishing our own worth or value within the workplace, we can start to change the misogynistic culture.

Yes, the term conspire tends to have a negative connotation associated with it. But in our case, we lovingly use the word conspire to acknowledge our work to bring about a certain outcome. Some would call this strategizing. While others may call it conniving. Can you guess which adjective is associated with each gender?

....

Women are finally feeling emboldened to own their truth.

....

So now that we've acknowledged the game for what it is, what are you going to do about it? It's time to live more boldly, to bolster up others with the understanding that a win for them is not a loss for you, but a win overall for women. There have been so many amazing things that have stemmed from the rise of the #MeToo movement. Women are finally feeling emboldened to own their truth, stop marginalizing their worth and understand that 'working while female' is not a death sentence for their career, but instead a platform to do better and be the change.

Meghan Anne Bunchman

Broadcast YOUR Beauty

Acknowledgments

As I finished the last chapter of this book my publisher asked me if I'd like to add an acknowledgments page. My initial reaction was to decline, because I felt like I poured so much of my heart and soul into this random experiment of a book that my mind was spent. But then I started to think about how my career, difficult and testing experiences and my story became my triumphant monologue all thanks to strong and like-minded women who took a chance on me. They took a chance by sharing with me their own vulnerabilities and stories so that I may learn from them and as I hope you will learn from me.

So here we go, thank you! Thank you to all those women (friends, acquaintances and complete strangers) who understand that a success for an individual female is a success for all of us. Thank you to those who have shifted their mindset, knowing that collaboration always trumps competition. Thank you to the she-bosses out there who have made it their mission to empower other females and build them up, specifically in male-dominated careers.

Meghan Anne Bunchman

Personally…

Thank You *Debra*, from the deepest parts of my soul for not only being a great mentor to me, but a dear friend. Your strength and commanding presence both on and off camera have been my guiding light of empowerment. Thank you for encouraging me to sit down and put pen to paper. This book wouldn't be an actual thing without you.

Angela, thank you. What a crazy and fun relationship we founded. You were my rock during a crazy time. Your grace and resoluteness is something I can only pray to one day achieve. Also, thank you for teaching me how to "smize."

Marley, my fellow girl boss. You are such an inspiration on how to achieve high levels of success both within your career and your personal relationships, while staying humble and kind. Your warmth and understanding of how to take control of your own life is truly something to be seen. I am blessed to call you a friend.

Thank you *Adriana* for bringing fun and laughter into not so ideal situations. Your faith and generosity inspire me every single day. I can't wait to see what life has in store for you next because I truly know and believe good things come to good people.

The conversation continues
on my podcast:
Broadcast Your Beauty.

Please like and subscribe!